CELEBRATING THE FAMILY NAME OF WILLIS

Celebrating the Family Name of Willis

Walter the Educator

Silent King Books
a WhichHead Entertainment Imprint

Celebrating the Family Name of Willis is a memory book that belongs to the Celebrating Family Name Book Series by Walter the Educator. Collect them all and more books at WaltertheEducator.com

USE THE EXTRA SPACE TO DOCUMENT YOUR FAMILY MEMORIES THROUGHOUT THE YEARS

WILLIS

Oh, name of Willis, steadfast and true,

With roots that stretch where dreams renew.

Your story weaves through time and space,

A tapestry rich with strength and grace.

Born of resilience, shaped by the land,

With hearts like rivers, steady and grand.

The Willises rise, no storm can subdue,

Their spirit, a beacon in skies of blue.

In every venture, they boldly tread,

With wisdom from those who've gone ahead.

Builders of futures, dreamers of more,

Guardians of love that forever soars.

The echo of Willis in laughter rings,

A name that triumph through struggle brings.

Carved in the winds, sung by the seas,

A harmony thriving on life's degrees.

Through fields they labor, through stars they steer,

The name of Willis stands bright and clear.

A heritage forged in the fires of fight,

With courage to conquer the endless night.

Each hand extended, each voice a song,

Together they flourish, together belong.

With roots entwined in earth's embrace,

The Willises thrive, no time can erase.

Guardians of kindness, their hearts aglow,

A family united, they ebb and flow.

Through trials they persevere, through joys they cheer,

A name that carries both love and fear.

From towering mountains to valleys below,

Their legacy travels where breezes go.

A symphony sung in whispers and roars,

A name that strides through history's doors.

Oh Willis, a name that shines like the sun,

In every endeavor, your work is done.

Through generations, your story unfolds,

A testament to the brave and bold.

So let us honor the name you bear,

A family bound by love and care.

The name of Willis, unshaken, will last,

A bridge from future to glorious past.

ABOUT THE CREATOR

Walter the Educator is one of the pseudonyms for Walter Anderson. Formally educated in Chemistry, Business, and Education, he is an educator, an author, a diverse entrepreneur, and he is the son of a disabled war veteran.
"Walter the Educator" shares his time between educating and creating. He holds interests and owns several creative projects that entertain, enlighten, enhance, and educate, hoping to inspire and motivate you.
Follow, find new works, and stay up to date with Walter the Educator™

at WaltertheEducator.com

9 798330 610990